Loves Adventures by Margaret Cavendish

Part II (of II)

Margaret Lucas Cavendish, Duchess of Newcastle-upon-Tyne was born in 1623 in Colchester, Essex into a family of comfortable means.

As the youngest of eight children she spent much time with her siblings. Margaret had no formal education but she did have access to scholarly libraries and tutors, although she later said the children paid little attention to the tutors, who were there 'rather for formality than benefit'.

From an early age Margaret was already assembling her thoughts for future works despite the then conditions of society that women did not partake in public authorship. For England it was also a time of Civil War. The Royalists were being pushed back and Parliamentary forces were in the ascendancy.

Despite these obvious dangers, when Queen Henrietta Maria was in Oxford, Margaret asked her mother for permission to become one of her Ladies-in-waiting. She was accepted and, in 1644, accompanied the Queen into exile in France. This took her away from her family for the first time.

Despite living at the Court of the young King Louis XIV, life for the young Margaret was not what she expected. She was far from her home and her confidence had been replaced by shyness and difficulties fitting in to the grandeur of her surroundings and the eminence of her company.

Margaret told her mother she wanted to leave the Court. Her mother was adamant that she should stay and not disgrace herself by leaving. She provided additional funds for her to make life easier. Margaret remained. It was now also that she met and married William Cavendish who, at the time, was the Marquis of Newcastle (and later Duke). He was also 30 years her senior and previously married with two children.

As Royalists, a return to life in England was not yet possible. They would remain in exile in Paris, Rotterdam and Antwerp until the restoration of the crown in 1660 although Margaret was able to return for attention to some estate matters.

Along with her husband's brother, Sir Charles Cavendish, she travelled to England after having been told that her husband's estate (taken from him due to his being a royalist) was to be sold and that she, as his wife, would receive some benefit of the sale. She received nothing. She left England to be with her husband again.

The couple were devoted to each other. Margaret wrote that he was the only man she was ever in love with, loving him not for title, wealth or power, but for merit, justice, gratitude, duty, and fidelity. She also relied upon him for support in her career. The marriage provided no children despite efforts made by her physician to overcome her inability to conceive.

Margaret's first book, 'Poems and Fancies', was published in 1653; it was a collection of poems, epistles and prose pieces which explores her philosophical, scientific and aesthetic ideas.

For a woman at this time writing and publishing were avenues they had great difficulty in pursuing. Added to this was Margaret's range of subjects. She wrote across a number of issues including gender, power, manners, scientific method, and philosophy.

She always claimed she had too much time on her hands and was therefore able to indulge her love of writing. As a playwright she produced many works although most are as closet dramas. (This is a play not intended to be performed onstage, but instead read by a solitary reader or perhaps out loud in a small group. For Margaret the rigours of exile, her gender and Cromwell's closing of the theatres mean this was her early vehicle of choice and, despite these handicaps, she became one of the most well-known playwrights in England)

Her utopian romance, 'The Blazing World', (1666) is one of the earliest examples of science fiction. Margaret also published extensively in natural philosophy and early modern science; at least a dozen books.

She was the first woman to attend a meeting at Royal Society of London in 1667 and she criticized and engaged with members and philosophers Thomas Hobbes, René Descartes, and Robert Boyle.

Margaret was always defended against any criticism by her husband and he also contributed to some of her works. She also gives him credit as her writing tutor.

Perhaps a little strangely she said her ambition despite her shyness, was to have everlasting fame. During her career, from the mid 1650's until her death, she was prolific. In recent decades her work has undergone a resurgence of interest propelled mainly by her ground-breaking attitude and accomplishments in those male straitened times.

Margaret Cavendish died on 15th December 1673 and was buried at Westminster Abbey.

Index of Contents

CAST LIST

The Lord Singularity
Sir Serious Dumb
Sir Timothy Complement
Sir Humphry Bold
Sir Roger Exception
Sir Peaceable Studious
Foster Trusty
Colonels, Captains, Lieutenants and Corporals
Petitioners
Officers
Messengers
Judges
Juries
Servants

The Lady Orphant
Lady Bashfull
Lady Ignorance
Lady Wagtaile
Lady Amorous
Nurse Fondly
Mrs Reformer, Lady Bashfulls woman
Chamber-maids.

ACT I

SCENE I

[Enter the Lady Bashfulls **CHAMBER-MAID**, and **MRS REFORMER** her woman.

MRS REFORMER
This dumb Lover is the most diligent'st servant that ever was, and methinks my Lady is somewhat more confident than she was; for she will sit and read whilst he sits by.

MAID
Doth she read to him?

MRS REFORMER
No, she reads to herself.

MAID
There comes abundance of Gallants to visit my Lady every day, and they have all one answer, that is, she is not willing to receive visits, and they all go civilly away, unless Sir Humphry Bold and he rails horribly.

MRS REFORMER
I have received from several Gentlemen, above 20. Letters a day, and as fast as they come, she makes me burn them.

MAID
But she reads them first.

MRS REFORMER
No, I read them to her.

MAID
And doth she answer all those Letters?

MRS REFORMER
She never answered one in her life, and I dare swear, she never will.

[The **LADY BASHFULL** calls, as within another Room.

MRS REFORMER
Madam!—

[Exeunt.

SCENE II

[Enter the **LORD SINGULARITY**, and **AFFECTIONATA**.

LORD SINGULARITY
Affectionata
Hast thou forgiven me my fault of doubting of thy vertue, so much as to put it to a Tryal.

AFFECTIONATA
My Noble Lord, have you forgiven my facility and wavering, faith that could so easily, and in so short a time believe you could be wicked, although you did accuse your self.

LORD SINGULARITY
Nay Affectionata, I did not accuse my self; though I did try thee.

AFFECTIONATA
Then I have committed a treble fault through my mistake, which requires a treble forgiveness.

LORD SINGULARITY
Thou art so vertuous, thou canst not commit a fault, and therefore needs no forgiveness.

[Exeunt.

SCENE III

[Enter the **LADY WAGTAILE**, and **SIR HUMPHREY BOLD**.

SIR HUMPHREY BOLD
Madam, You have been pleased to profess a friendship to me, and I shall desire you will do a friendly part for me.

LADY WAGTAILE
Any thing that lyes in my power, good Sir Humphry Bold.

SIR HUMPHREY BOLD
Then pray, Madam, speak to the Lady Bashfull in my behalf, that I may be her Husband.

LADY WAGTAILE

I will Sir Humphry, but she is bashfull, yet I was there Yesterday, and she entertained me indifferently well, but seemed to be wonderfull coy; but howsoever I will do my poor indeavour, Sir Humphry.

SIR HUMPHREY BOLD
Pray do, Madam.

[Exeunt.

SCENE IV

[Enter **AFFECTIONATA**, walking in a melancholly posture; his Hat pulled over his brows, and his arms inter-folded; To him enters the **LORD SINGULARITY**.

LORD SINGULARITY
My Affectionata, Why walks thou so melancholly?

[He pulls of his Hat to his **LORD**, and bows.

AFFECTIONATA
The cause is not that I lye under an aspersion, by reason I lye not under a crime; But truly, my Lord, I am troubled that I am threatened to be tormented, for I would not willingly indure pain, though I could willingly receive death; but as for the aspersions, I am no wayes concerned; for I make no question, but my honest life, my just actions, and the truth of my words, will so clear me at the last, as I shall appear as innocent to the World, as Angels doth in Heaven.

LORD SINGULARITY
Comfort your self, for I will rather suffer death, than you shall suffer pain.

AFFECTIONATA
Heaven defend you, my Lord, whatsoever I suffer,

[Exit.

SCENE V

[Enter the **LADY WAGTAILE**, and **MRS REFORMER**.

LADY WAGTAILE
Pray Mistriss Reformer, be Sir Humphry Bold 's friend to thy Lady, and I protest to thee, he shall be thy friend, as long as he and you live, and I do not see any reason your Lady should refuse him: for he is both as proper and stout a man, as any is living this day in the Land.

MRS REFORMER

Indeed Madam, I dare not mention it to my Lady, for she is so adverse against marriage, as she takes those for her enemies as doth but mention it.

LADY WAGTAILE

Then surely she is not a woman, for there is none of the effeminate Sex, but takes it for a disgrace to live an old maid, and rather than dye one, they will marry any man that will have them; and the very fear of not marrying, is so terrible to them, as whilst they are so young, as they are not fit to make wives, they will miserably cast away themselves to the first that makes a proffer, although they be poor, base or mean, rather than venture to try out their fortunes.

MRS REFORMER

But my Lady is not of that humour.

LADY WAGTAILE

Come, come, I know thou canst perswade thy Lady if thou wouldst, and if you will, Sir Humphry Bold will give thee 500 l. to buy thee a Husband, for thou hast lived too long a maid I faith.

MRS REFORMER

I am not a maid, Madam, I am a widow.

LADY WAGTAILE

What, a musty widow!

MRS REFORMER

I know not whether I am musty, but I am a widow.

LADY WAGTAILE

Let mee tell thee, that it is as great a disgrace to live a widow, as an old maid; wherefore take thee 500 l. to get thee a second Husband.

MRS REFORMER

Truly I would not sell my Lady for all the World, much less, for 500 l. neither would I marry again, if I were young, and might have my choyce.

LADY WAGTAILE

Lord bless me, and send me out of this house, least it should infect me; for let me tell thee, were my Husband dead to morrow, I would marry the day after his Funeral, if I could get any man to marry me, and so I would serve 20. Husbands one after another.

MRS REFORMER

Your best way were to have 20. Husbands at one time, so that your Ladyship might not be a day without.

LADY WAGTAILE

O fie! If women might have twenty Husbands, they would have no room for courtly Servants; but prithy help Sir Humphry Bold, and take his offer, and let me speak with the Lady myself.

MRS REFORMER

That your Ladyship cannot at this time, for my Lady is not well.

LADY WAGTAILE
Then pray remember my most humble service, and tell her, I will come to morrow, and if she be sick, I will talk her well.

[**LADY WAGTAILE** Exit.

[**MRS REFORMER** alone.

MRS REFORMER
Dead you would talk her, for thou hast an endless tongue; Oh! what man is so miserable that is her Husband.

[**MRS REFORMER** Exit.

SCENE VI

[Enter **TWO** or **THREE COMMANDERS**.

1ST COMMANDER
It is reported that our Generals Page hath behaved himself so handsomly, spoke so wittily, defended his cause so prudently, declared his innocence so clearly, and carried his business so wisely, as the Venetian States have not only quitted him freely, but doth applaud him wonderfully, extolls him highly, and offers him any satisfaction for the injurie and disgrace that hath been done him; but he only desires, that the man that had accused him, which man, was one of the Generals men, should be pardoned, and not punished.

2ND COMMANDER
I hope our General is well pleased, that his beloved boy is not only cleared, but applauded.

1ST COMMANDER
O! He doth nothing but imbrace him, and kiss him, as if he were his only son, yet he did gently chide him that he asked pardon for his accusers; for said he, if all false accusers should be pardoned, no honest man would escape free from censure.

3RD COMMANDER
But I hear the States have given order to our General to meet the Turkes again, for it is reported by intelligences that they have recruited into a numerous body.

2ND COMMANDER
Faith I think the Turkes are like the tale of the Gyant, that when his head was cut off there rise two in the place.

1ST COMMANDER
I think they are like the vegetable that is named threefold, the more it is cut the faster it growes.

3RD COMMANDER
I would the Devil had them for me.

2ND COMMANDER
We do what we can to send them to Hell; but whether they will quit thee, I cannot tell.

[Exeunt.

[Enter the **LORD SINGULARITY**, and **AFFECTIONATA**.

LORD SINGULARITY
My Affectionata I wonder you could suffer an accusation so patiently knowing you were accused falsly.

AFFECTIONATA
The clearnesse of my innocency needed not the fury of a violent passion to defend it, neither could passion have rectified an injury.

LORD SINGULARITY
Tis true, yet passion is apt to rise in defence of innocency, and honour.

AFFECTIONATA
And many times passion (my Lord) destroyes the life in striving to maintaine the truth, and defend the innocent; but I find a passionate sorrow that your Lordship must go to indanger your life in the warrs again.

LORD SINGULARITY
The warrs is pastime to me, for I hate idlenesse, and no imployment pleases me better than fighting, so it be in a good cause, but you shall stay.

AFFECTIONATA
Why my Lord, are you weary of my service?

LORD SINGULARITY
Know I am carefull of thy safety, thy rest and peace, for shouldst thou not come near danger, yet the very tragical aspect will terrefie thee to death, thou art of so tender a nature, so soft and sweet a disposition.

AFFECTIONATA
Truly my Lord, if you leave me behind you, the very fear of your life will kill me, where if your Lordyship will let me go, love will give me courage.

LORD SINGULARITY

Then let me tell you, you must not go, for I have adopted you my Son, and I have setled all my Estate upon thee, where, if I am killed, you shall be my Heir, for I had rather vertue should inherit my Estate than birth, yet I charge thee take my Name upon thee, as well as my Estate unto thee.

AFFECTIONATA
My noble Lord, I should be prouder to bear your name, than to be Master of the whole World; but I shall never be so base to keep my self in safety, in hope of your Estate, wherefore must intreat your leave to go with you.

LORD SINGULARITY
I will not give you leave, but command you to the contrary, which is to stay.

AFFECTIONATA
I cannot obey you in this, for love will force me to run after you.

LORD SINGULARITY
I will have you lash'd, if you offer to go.

AFFECTIONATA
Stripes cannot stay me!

LORD SINGULARITY
I will have you tyed, and kept by force.

AFFECTIONATA
By Heaven, my Lord, i'l tear my flesh, and break my bones to get lose, and if I have not legs to run, i'l creep thorough the Earth like worms, for though I shall move but slowly, yet it will be a satisfaction to my soul, that I am travelling after you,

LORD SINGULARITY
Affectionata, You anger me very much.

AFFECTIONATA
Indeed my Lord, you grieve me more than I can anger you.

[**AFFECTIONATA** weeps.

LORD SINGULARITY
What, do you crie! and yet desire to be a souldier?

AFFECTIONATA
A valiant heart, my Lord, may have a weeping eye to keep it company.

LORD SINGULARITY
If no perswasion can stay you, you must go along with me.

[**AFFECTIONATA** bows, as giving his **LORD SINGULARITY** thanks.

Exeunt.

SCENE VIII

[Enter the **LADY WAGTAILE**, the **LADY AMOROUS, SIR HUMPHREY BOLD, SIR TIMOTHY COMPLEMENT**, to the **LADY BASHFULL**, who hangs down her head, as out of countenance.

LADY WAGTAILE
Faith Lady Bashfull, we will have you abroad to Balls and publick meetings, to learn you a confident behaviour, and a bold speech; Fie! You must not be bashfull.

LADY AMOROUS
Our visiting her sometimes, hath made her so, as she is not altogether so bashfull as she was.

[Enter **SIR SERIOUS DUMB**, who bows first to the **LADY BASHFULL**, then to the rest of the **COMPANY**, and then goeth behind the **LADY BASHFULL**, and stands close by **MRS REFORMER**.

LADY AMOROUS
Surely Sir Serious Dumb is a domestick servant here, he stands and waits as one.

[He bows with an acknowledging face.

SIR HUMPHREY BOLD
If she wil entertain such servants as he, she is not so modest as she appears. Lady, perchance if I had come privately alone, I had been entertained with more freedom, and not have had my suit denied, and my person neglected with scorn, and he received with respect.

[**SIR SERIOUS DUMB** comes and gives him a box on the eare, they both draw their swords, all the WOMEN runs away squeeking, only the **LADY BASHFULL** stayes, and runs betwixt their swords, and parts them; **SIR TIMOTHY COMPLEMENT** looks on as afraid to stir.

LADY BASHFULL
For Heaven sake! fight not here, to affright me with your quarrels.

SIR HUMPHREY BOLD
I will have his heart-bloud.

LADY BASHFULL
Good Sir Serious Dumb, and Sir Humphry Bold, leave off fighting.

[**SIR SERIOUS DUMB** draws back.

LADY BASHFULL
Pray Sir Humphry Bold, give me your sword, that I may be sure you will not fight.

SIR HUMPHREY BOLD

What, yield my sword up! I will dye first.

[Enter the **LADIES** again.

[**ALL** speak at one time.

—who is kill'd, who is kill'd.

[**SIR HUMPHREY BOLD** presses towards **SIR SERIOUS DUMB**.

LADY BASHFULL
Good Ladies, hold Sir Humphry Bold, and I will try to perswade Sir Serious Dumb.

[They hold **SIR HUMPHREY BOLD**.

LADY WAGTAILE
What, you shall not stir, I am sure you will not oppose us women.

LADY BASHFULL
Noble Sir, to give me an assurance you will not fight, give me your sword.

[**SIR SERIOUS DUMB** kisses the hilt of his sword, then gives it her.

[**SIR HUMPHREY BOLD** gets lose from the **LADIES**, and goeth to assault **SIR SERIOUS DUMB**; He being unarmed, the **LADY BASHFULL** seeing him, steps betwixt them, and with Sir Serious Dumb's sword, strikes at **SIR HUMPHREY BOLD**, and strikes his sword out of his hand.

LADY BASHFULL
What, are you not ashamed to assault an unarmed man.

[**SIR HUMPHREY BOLD** runs to take up his sword, she also runs and sets her foot upon it.

LADY BASHFULL
Let the sword alone, for it is my prize; and by Heaven, if you touch it, I will run you thorough with this sword in my hand.

[**SIR HUMPHREY BOLD** runs, and catcheth Sir Timothy Compliments sword, and offers to make a thrust at **SIR SERIOUS DUMB**, who puts the sword by, and beats it down with one hand, and with the other strikes it aside, then closes with him, and being skillfull at Wrestling, trips up his heels, then gets upon him, and having both his hands at liberty, wrings out Sir Humphry Bold 's sword out of his hand, then ariseth and gives the sword to the right owner, who all the time trembled for fear, and never durst strive to part them.

[The **WOMEN** in the mean time squeeks.

SIR HUMPHREY BOLD
Hell take me, but I will be revenged: Lady, I hope you will give me my sword again.

LADY BASHFULL

Never to fight against a woman, but my victorious spoils, I will deliver to this gallant Gentleman, who delivered up his life and honour into my hand, when he gave me his sword, and I indangered the loss of both by taking it, for which my gratitude hath nothing to return him but my self and fortunes, if he please to accept of that and me.

[**SIR SERIOUS DUMB** bows with a respect, and kisses her hand.

LADY BASHFULL

Sir, I wish my person were more beautifull than it is, for your sake, and my fortune greater, with more certainty of continuance, as neither being subject to time or accident, but this certainly I will promise you, which is, my chaste and honest life; Now Sir, pray take these two swords, this was yours, fear gave me confidence, this I won, love gave me courage.

[Gives him the two swords.

[**SIR SERIOUS DUMB** leads out his **MISTRISS**.

[Exit.

SIR HUMPHREY BOLD

I will be revenged.

[**OMNES** Exeunt.

ACT II

SCENE I

[Enter the **LORD SINGULARITY**, and **AFFECTIONATA**.

LORD SINGULARITY

Affectionata, I hear thou hast bought Arms, I am sure thou canst not fight.

AFFECTIONATA

I am sure I will do my indeavour, my Lord.

LORD SINGULARITY

Why, the very weight of thy Arms will sink thee down.

AFFECTIONATA

O no, my Lord, my desire shall bear them up.

LORD SINGULARITY

Alas, thou hast no strength to fight?

AFFECTIONATA

What strength my active body wants, my vigorous spirits shall make good.

LORD SINGULARITY

Prethee, my boy, do not adventure thy self, but stay in my Tent.

AFFECTIONATA

That would be a shame for me, and a dishonour to you, since you have adopted me your son, wherefore the World shall never say, you have bestowed your favour and your love upon a coward.

LORD SINGULARITY

I well perceive I have adopted a very willfull boy?

AFFECTIONATA

Indeed, my Lord, I have no will, but what doth follow you.

[The **GENERAL** strokes **AFFECTIONATA** on the cheek.

[Exeunt.

SCENE II

[Enter **SIR SERIOUS DUMB**, and his Mistriss the **LADY BASHFULL**.

SIR SERIOUS DUMB

The time I vowed to silence is expir'd, and though my thoughts not gloriously attired with Eloquence, for Rhetorick I have none, yet civil words, fit for to wait upon a modest Lady, and to entertain an honest mind with words of truth, though plain? For 'tis not Rhetorick makes a happy life, but sweet society, that's void of strife.

LADY BASHFULL

Sir, Rhetorick is rather for sound than sense, for words than reason.

SIR SERIOUS DUMB

Yet my sweet Mistriss, I wish my voice were tuned to your eare, and every word set as a pleasing note to make such musick as might delight your mind.

LADY BASHFULL

Your words flow thorough my ears, as smooth, clear, pure water from the spring of Hellicon, which doth not only refresh, but inrich my dull insipid brain.

SCENE III

[Enter a **CAPTAIN** and his **CORPORAL**.

CORPORAL
The Turks never received such a blow, as they have this time?

CAPTAIN
A pox of them, they have made us sweat?

CORPORAL
Why Captain, sweating will cure the Pox, and though you curse the Turks, yet it is we that live in Italy, that is diseased with them.

CAPTAIN
The truth is, we lost more health in the Venetian service, than we gain wealth.

CORPORAL
Nay faith Captain, we do not only lose our health, but wast our wealth, for what booties we get from the Turks, the Courtezans gets from us.

CAPTAIN
For that cause now I have gotten a good bootie, I will return into mine own Country, and buy a—

CORPORAL
A what Captain?

CAPTAIN
An Office in civil Government.

CORPORAL
But you will never be civil in your Office.

CAPTAIN
That needs not to be, for though all Magisterial Offices bears a civil Authority, yet the Officers and Magistrates therein, are more cruel and ravenons than common souldiers.

CORPORAL
Verily Captain, I think common Souldiers are more mercifull and just than they.

CAPTAIN
Verely Corporal, I think you will become a Puritan Preacher.

CORPORAL
Why should you think so, Captain.

CAPTAIN
First, because you have got the Pox, and that will make you Preach in their tone, which is, to speak thorough the nose; the next is, you have left the ranting Oaths that Souldiers use to swear, and use their phrases; as verily my beloved brethren, which brethrens souls, they care not for, nor thinks thereof, for though they speak to the brethren, they Preach to the sisters, which edifies wonderfully by their

Doctrine, and they gain and receive as wonderfull from their female flocks, for those Puritan Preachers have more Tithes out of the Marriage-bed, than from the Parish-stock.

CORPORAL
If it be so beneficial, Captain, I had rather be a Puritan Preacher, than an Atheistical States-man.

CAPTAIN
Faith Corporal, I think there is not much Religion in either, but if there be, it lies in the States-man, for he keep; Peace, the other makes War.

CORPORAL
If they make wars, they are our friends, for we live by the spoils of our enemies.

CAPTAIN
'Tis true, when as we get a victory, or else our enemies lives on the spoil of us, for though we have no goods to lose, yet we venture our lives, neither do we live on the spoil of our enemies, but only in forreign wars, for in civil wars we live by the spoil of our Friends, and the ruining of our Country.

CORPORAL
Then we are only obliged to Preachers for civil wars.

CAPTAIN
Faith Corporal, we are obliged to them for both; for as their factious Doctrine causes a Rebellion by railing on the Governours and Governments, so their flattering Sermons sets a Prince on fire, who burns in hot ambition to conquer all the World.

CORPORAL
These latter Preachers you mention, Captain, are not Puritan Preachers, but Royal Preachers.

CAPTAIN
You are right Corporal, for they are divided in two parts, although their Doctrine meets at one end, which is in war.

CORPORAL
Captain, you have discovered so fully of Preachers, that if you will give me leave, I will preach to our Company.

CAPTAIN
Out you rogue, will you raise a war amongst our selves, causing a mutinie to cut one anothers throats?

CORPORAL
Why Captain, it is the fashion and practice for Souldiers to Preach now adayes.

CAPTAIN
That is amongst the Rebel party to keep up their faction, and to strengthen the flank thereof, but amongst the Royal party, the Preaching Ministers turn fighting Souldiers, incouraging with their good example, as by their valliant onsets, and not the Souldiers Preaching Ministers.

CORPORAL

Why Captain, the Royal party needs no incouragement, the justice of their cause is sufficient.

CAPTAIN

You say right, they want not courage to fight, but they want conscience to plunder; Besides, the Royal party is apt to give quarter, which should not be, for Souldiers should destroy all they take in Civil-wars, by reason there is no gain to be made of their Prisoners, as by the way of Ransoms, but if we stay from our Company, our General will preach such a Sermon, as may put us into despair of his favour, and indanger our lives at the Council of war.

[Exeunt.

SCENE IV

[Enter **THREE** or **FOUR COMMANDERS**.

1ST COMMANDER

I think our Generals new made son is a spirit; for when the General was surrounded with the Turks, this adopted Son of his flew about like lightening, and made such a massacre of the Turks, as they lay as thick upon the ground, as if they had been mushromes.

2ND COMMANDER

Certainly the General had been taken Prisoner, if his Son had not rescued him, for the General had adventure too far into the enemies body.

1ST COMMANDER

'Tis strange, and doth amaze me with wonder, to think how such a Willow-twig could bore so many mortal holes in such strong timber'd bodies as the Turks.

2ND COMMANDER

By him one would believe miracles were not ceast.

3RD COMMANDER

Well, for my part I will ask pardon of my General for condemning him privately in my thoughts, for I did think him the most fond, (I will not say what) for adopting a poor Beggar-boy for his son, and setled all his Estate, which is, a very great one upon him.

1ST COMMANDER

The truth is, he is a very gallant youth, and if he lives and continues in the wars, he will prove a most excellent Souldier.

2ND COMMANDER

Certainly he sprung from a Noble Stock, either by his Fathers side, or by his Mothers.

1ST COMMANDER

By his behaviour he seems Nobly born from both.

3RD COMMANDER
And by his poverty, Nobly born from neither.

1ST COMMANDER
Mean persons may have wealth, and Noble births be Beggars.

[Exeunt.

[Enter **AFFECTIONATA** in brave cloths, Hat and Feather, and a Sword by his side, and a great many **COMMANDERS** following and attending him, with their Hats off, the whilst he holds off his Hat to them.

AFFECTIONATA
Gentlemen, I beseech you, use not this ceremonie to me, it belongs only to my Lord General.

COMMANDERS
Your merits and gallant actions deserves it from us; Besides, it is your due, as being the Generals adopted Son.

AFFECTIONATA
My Lords favour may place a value on me, though I am poor in worth, and no wayes deserves this respect.

1ST COMMANDER
Faith Sir, had it not been for you, we had lost the battel.

AFFECTIONATA
Alas, my weak arm could never make a conquest, although my will was good, and my desire strong to do a service.

2ND COMMANDER
Sir, the service was great, when you rescued our General, for when a General is taken or kill'd, the Armies are put to rout, for then the common Souldiers runs away, never stayes to fight it out.

AFFECTIONATA
I beseech you Gentlemen, take not the honour from my Lord to give it me, for he was his own defence, and ruine to his enemies; for his valiant spirits shot thorouh his eyes, and struck them dead, thus his own courage was his own safety, and the Venetians victory.

[Enter a **MESSENGER** from the Venetian-States to **AFFECTIONATA**, he bows to him.

MESSENGER
Noble Sir, the Venetian -States hath made you Lieutenant-General of the whole Armie, and one of the Council of War, where they desire your presence.

AFFECTIONATA
The honours they have given me, is beyond my management.

[**MESSENGER** Exit.

[As **AFFECTIONATA** was going forth, enters some poor **SOULDIERS WIVES** with Petitions, offers to present them to **AFFECTIONATA**.

1ST WIFE
Good your Honour, speak in the behalf of my Petition.

2ND WIFE
And mine.

3RD WIFE
And mine.

AFFECTIONATA
Good women, I cannot do you service, for if your Petitions are just, my Lord the General will grant your request, and if they be unjust, he will not be unjust in granting them for my intreatie, nor will I intreat therefore.

WIVES
If it please your Honour, we implore Mercy, not Justice.

AFFECTIONATA
Where Justice and Wisdom will give leave for Mercy, I am sure my Lord will grant it, otherwise, what you call mercy, will prove cruelty, and cause ruine and destruction.

WIVES
We beseech your Honour then, but to deliver our Petitions.

AFFECTIONATA
For what are they?

WIVES
For the lives of our Husbands.

AFFECTIONATA
Are they to be executed?

WIVES
They are condemned, and to be hanged to morrow, unless the General gives them pardons.

AFFECTIONATA
What are their crimes?

1ST WIFE
My Husband is to be hanged for plundering a few old rotten Houshold-goods.

AFFECTIONATA
Give me your Petition, necessity might inforce him.

2ND WIFE
My Husband is to be hanged for disobeying his Captain when he was drunk.

AFFECTIONATA
When which was drunk? your Husband or his Captain?

WIFE
My Husband.

AFFECTIONATA
Disobedience ought to be severely punished, yet because his reason was drowned in his drink, and his understanding smothered with the vapour thereof, whereby he knew not what he did, I will deliver your Petition.

AFFECTIONATA
And what is yours?

3RD WIFE
My Husband is to be hanged for ravishing a Virgin.

AFFECTIONATA
I will never deliver a Petition for those that are Violaters of Virginity, I will sooner act the Hang-mans part my self to strangle him.
[To **ANOTHER WIFE**]
And what is your Husbands crime?

4TH WIFE
My Husband is to be hanged for murther.

AFFECTIONATA
O horrid! They that murther, ought to have no mercy given to them, since they could give no mercy to others.

WIVES
Good your Honour.

AFFECTIONATA
Nay, never press me, for I will never deliver your Petition.

[**WIVES** Exeunt.

[Enter **COMMANDERS** that were to be Cashiered to Petition **AFFECTIONATA**.

1ST CAPTAIN
Noble Sir, I come to intreat you to be my friend, to speak to the General in my behalf, that I may remain in my place, for I am to be cashierd.

AFFECTIONATA
For what?

1ST CAPTAIN
For a small fault, Sir, for when the battel was begun, I had such a cholick took me in the stomach, as I was forced to go aside, and untruss a point.

AFFECTIONATA
It had been more for your honour, Captain, to had let nature discharge it self in your breeches. And what, are you cashiered Captain?

2ND CAPTAIN
Marry, for my good service, for when the battel begun, my Souldiers run away, and I run after to call them back, they run, and I rid so long, as we were gotten ten miles from the Armie, but I could not get them, untill such time as the battel was won.

AFFECTIONATA
It had been more honour for you to have fought single alone without your Souldiers, than to have followed your Souldiers, although to make them stay, and you would have done more service with your standing still than your running; and what, are you to be cashiered?

3RD CAPTAIN
Why Sir, my company wanted Powder, and I went to fetch or give order; for some to be brought, and before I returned to my Company, the battel was won.

AFFECTIONATA
It had been more for your honour and good service, to have stayed and incouraged your Souldiers by your example with fighting with your sword, for the sword makes a greater execution than the shot; but since they were not wilfull, nor malicious faults, I shall do you what service I can, for fear sometimes may seize the valiantest man. And what were your faults Colonel?

1ST COLONEL
Mine was for betraying a Fort.

AFFECTIONATA
O base! He that betrays a Fort, ventures to betray a Kingdom, which is millions of degrees worse than to betray a life, or a particular friend; for those that betrays a Kingdom, betrays numbers of lifes, and those that betrays their native Country, betrays that which gave them nourishing strength, and you have had great mercy in giving you your life, although you lose your place. And what was your fault?

COMMANDER
Mine was for neglecting the Watch.

AFFECTIONATA
That is as bad as to give leave for the enemie to surprize, only the one betrays through carelesness, the other through covetousness. And what was your fault Colonel?

COLONEL
Mine was for disobeying the Generals Orders.

AFFECTIONATA
Let me tell you Colonel, he that will not obey, is not fit to command; and those that commits careless, stubborn, malicious and wicked crimes; I will never deliver their Petition, nor speak in their behalf.

[**COMMANDERS** Exeunt.

[Enter a poor **SOULDIER**.

SOULDIER
Good your Honour save me from punishment.

AFFECTIONATA
What are you to be punished for?

SOULDIER
I am to be punished, because I said my Captain was a coward.

AFFECTIONATA
What reason had you to say so?

SOULDIER
The reason was, because he sung and whistled when he went to fight.

AFFECTIONATA
That might be to shew his courage.

SOULDIER
O no, it was to hide his fear.

AFFECTIONATA
But you ought not to have called your Captain coward, had he been so; for the faults of Superiours are to be winked at, and obscured, and not to be divulged: Besides, yours was but a supposition, unless he ran away.

SOULDIER
No Sir, he fought.

AFFECTIONATA
Then you were too blame for judging so.

SOULDIER

confess it, Sir, wherefore pray speak for me.

AFFECTIONATA
Indeed I cannot, for to call a man coward, is to kill, at least to wound his reputation, which is far worse, than if you had kill'd the life of his body; by how much honour is to be preferred before life; but if you can make your peace with your Captain by asking his pardon; I will then speak to the General, that the sentence for your punishment may be taken off, wherefore let me advise you to go to your Captain, and in the most humblest and sorrowfulst manner ask forgiveness of him.

SOULDIER
I shall, and it please your Honour.

[Exeunt.

SCENE VI

[Enter **SIR PEACEABLE STUDIOUS** solus.

SIR PEACEABLE STUDIOUS
How happy is a private life to me;
Wherein my thoughts ran easily and free;
And not disturb'd with vanities and toyes,
On which the senses gazes, as young boys
On watery bubbles in the aire blown,
Which when they break, doth vanish and are gone.

[Enter the **LADY IGONRANCE**.

LADY IGNORANCE
I doubt I disturb your Poetry?

SIR PEACEABLE STUDIOUS
No wife, you rather give life and fire to my muse, being chaste, fair and vertuous, which are the chief theams for Poets fancies to work on.

LADY IGNORANCE
But that wife that is despised by her Husband, and not loved, is dejected in her own thoughts, and her mind is so disquietted, as it masks her beauty, and vails, and obscures her vertues.

SIR PEACEABLE STUDIOUS
The truth is, wife, that if my affections to you, had not been firmly setled; your indiscretion and effeminate follies had ruined it, but my love is so true, as you have no cause to be jealouse; but I confess you made me sad, to think that your humour could not sympathize with mine, as to walk in the same course of life as I did, but you were ignorant and would not believe me, untill you had found experience by practice, by which practice you have found my words to be true, do you not?

LADY IGNORANCE

Yes, so true, as I shall never doubt them more; But pray Husband, tell me what discourse you had with the Ladies, when you went abroad with them?

SIR PEACEABLE STUDIOUS

Why, they railed against good Husbands, called them Uxorious Fools, Clowns, Blocks, Stocks, and that they were only fit to be made Cuckolds through their confident fondness, and that kind Husbands appeared like simple Asses; I answered, that those Husbands that were Cuckolds, appeared not only like silly Asses, but base Cowards, that would suffer their wives to be courted, and themselves dishonoured when they ought to destroy their wives Gallants, if visibly known, and to part from their wives, at least to inancor them, and not only for being false, but for the suspition caused by their indiscretions; otherwise said I, a kind Husband shews himself a Gallant, Noble, Generous, Just, Wise man, and contrary, he is a base man, that will strive to disgrace himself, by disgracing his wife with neglects and disrespects; and a coward, to tyranize only over the weak, tender, and helpless Sex; for women being tender, shiftless, and timorous creatures by nature, is the cause they joyn themselves by chaste Wedlock to us men for their safety, protection, honour and livelyhood, and when a man takes a woman to his wife, he is an unworthy and treacherous person, if he betrays her to scorns, or yields her to scoffs, or leaves her to poverty; and he is a base man that makes his wife sigh and weep with unkindness either by words or actions, wherefore said I, it is wisdom for men to respect their wives with a civil behaviour, and sober regard, and it is heroick to defend, protect and guard their lives and vertues, to be constant to their vows, promises and protestations, and it is generous to cherish their health, to attend them in their sickness, to comply with their harmless humours, to entertain their discourses, to accompany their persons, to yield to their lawfull desires, and to commend their good graces, and that man which is a Husband, and doth not do thus, is worthy to be shamed, and not to be kept company with, which is not called an Uxorious Husband; for said I, an Uxorious Husband I understand to be, a honest, carefull and wise Husband.

LADY IGNORANCE

And what said they, after you said this?

SIR PEACEABLE STUDIOUS

They laugh'd and said, my flowery Rhetorick was strewed upon a dirty ground; I answered, it was not dirty where I lived, for my wife was beautifull, chaste and cleanly, and I wished every man the like, and after they perceived that neither the railing, nor laughing at good Husbands could not temper me for their palats, they began to play and sport with one another, and sung wanton songs, and when all their baits failed, they quarreled with me, and said I was uncivil, and that I did not entertain them well, and that I was not good Company, having not a conversable wit, nor a gentle behaviour, and that I was not a gallant Cavalier, and a world of those reproches and idle discourses, as it would tire me to repeat it, and you to hear it.

LADY IGNORANCE

Pray resolve me one question more, what was it you said to the Lady Amorous, when she threatned to tell me?

SIR PEACEABLE STUDIOUS

I only said nature was unkind to our Sex, in making the beautifull females cruel.

LADY IGNORANCE

Was that all, I thought you had pleaded as a courtly Sutor for loves favours.

SIR PEACEABLE STUDIOUS
No indeed, but let me tell you, and so inform you, wife, that those humour'd women, take as great a pleasure to make wives jealousie of their Husbands, and Husbands jealouse of their wives, and to separate their affections, and to make a disorder in their Families, as to plot and design to intice men to court them, & Cuckold their Husband, also let me tell you, that much company, and continual resort, brings great inconveniences for its apt to corrupt the mind, and make the thoughts wild, the behaviour bold, the words vain, the discourse either flattering, rude or tedious, their actions extravagant, their persons cheap, being commonly occompanyed, or their company common. Besides, much variety of Company, creates amorous luxurie, vanity, prodigality, jealousie, envie, malice, slander, envie, treachery, quarrels, revenge and many other evils, as laying plots to insnare the Honourable, to accuse the Innocent, to deceive the Honest, to corrupt the Chaste, to deboyst the Temperate, to pick the purse of the Rich, to inslave the poor, to pull down lawfull Authority, and to break just Laws; but when a man lives to himself within his own Familie, and without recourse, after a solitary manner, he lives free, without controul, not troubled with company, but entertains himself with himself, which makes the soul wise, the mind sober, the thoughts industrious, the understanding learned, the heart honest, the senses quiet, the appetites temperate, the body healthfull, the actions just and prudent, the behaviour civil and sober; He governs orderly, eats peaceably, sleeps quietly, lives contentedly, and most commonly, plentifully and pleasantly, ruling and governing his little Family to his own humour, wherein he commands with love, and is obeyed with duty, and who that is wise, and is not mad, would quit this heavenly life to live in hellish Societies, and what can an honest Husband and wife desire more, than love, peace and plenty, and when they have this, and is not content, 'tis a sign they stand upon a Quagmire, or rotten Foundation, that will never hold or indure, that is, they are neither grounded on honesty, nor supported with honour.

LADY IGNORANCE
Well Husband, I will not interupt your studies any longer, but as you study Phylosophie, Wisdom and Invention, so I will study obedience, discretion and Houswifery.

[**OMNES** Exeunt.

ACT III

SCENE I

[Enter the **GENERAL**, and **AFFECTIONATA**.

LORD SINGULARITY
Affectionata, Were you never bred to the Discipline of War?

AFFECTIONATA
Never, my Lord, but what I have been since I came to you.

LORD SINGULARITY

Why, thou didst speak at the Council of War, as if thou hadst been an old experienced souldier, having had the practice of fourty years, which did so astonish the grave Senators and old Souldiers, that they grew dumb, and for a while did only gaze on thee.

AFFECTIONATA
Indeed, my Lord, my young years, and your grave Counsel did not suit together.

LORD SINGULARITY
But let me tell thee, my boy, thy rational and wise speeches, and that grave counsels was not mis-match'd.

AFFECTIONATA
Pray Heaven I may prove so, as your favours, and your love may not be thought misplaced.

LORD SINGULARITY
My Love thinks thee worthy of more than I can give thee, had I more power than Cæsar had.

[Exeunt.

SCENE II

[Enter some **COMMANDERS**.

1ST COMMANDER
I hear that the Duke of Venice is so taken with our Generals adopted Son, as he will adopt him his Son.

2ND COMMANDER
Hay-day! I have heard that a Father hath had many Sons, but never that one Son hath had so many Fathers; but contrary, many Sons wants fathering.

3RD COMMANDER
'Tis true, some Sons hath the misfortune not to be owned, but let me tell you Lieutenant, there be few children that hath not many such Fathers; as one begets a childe, a second owns the childe, a third keeps the childe, which inherits as the right Heir; and if a fourth will adopt the childe; a fift, or more may do the like, if they please.

1ST COMMANDER
So amongst all his Fathers, the right Father is lost.

3RD COMMANDER
Faith, the right Father of any childe is seldome known, by reason that women takes as much delight in deceiving the World, and dissembling with particular men, as in the cuckolding their Husbands.

2ND COMMANDER
The truth is, every several Lover cuckolds one another.

1ST COMMANDER
Perchance that is the reason that women strives to have so many Lovers; for women takes pleasure to make Cuckolds.

3RD COMMANDER
And Cuckolds to own children.

[Exeunt.

SCENE III

[Enter **AFFECTIONATA**, then enters to him, **TWO** or **THREE VENETIAN GENTLEMEN**, as Embassadors from the Duke of Venice.

1ST GENTLEMAN
Noble Sir, the great Duke of Venice hath sent us to let you know he hath adopted you his Son, and desires your company.

AFFECTIONATA
Pray return the great Duke thanks, and tell him those favours are too great for such a one as I; but if he could, and would adopt me, as Augustus Cæsar did Tiberius, and make me master of the whole World; by Heaven I would refuse it, and rather chose to live in a poor Cottage, with my most Noble Lord.

2ND GENTLEMAN
But you must not deny him; Besides, he will have you.

AFFECTIONATA
I will dye first, and rather chose to bury my self in my own tears, than build a Throne with ingratitude.

1ST GENTLEMAN
But it is ungratefull to deny the Duke.

AFFECTIONATA
O no, but I should be the ingrate of ingratitude, should I leave my Noble Lord, who from a low despised poor mean degree, advanced me to Respect and Dignity:
Whose favours I will keep close in my heart,
And from his person I will never part.
For though I dye, my soul will still attend,
And Wait upon him, as his faithfull friend.

[He offers to go away in a melancholly posture and humour, so as not considering the **GENTLEMEN**. Whereupon one of them follows him, and catches hold of his Cloak.

2ND GENTLEMAN
Noble Sir, will not you send the Duke an answer?

AFFECTIONATA
Have not I answered? Then pray present my thanks in the most humblest manner to the great Duke, and tell him he may force the presence of my person, but if he doth, it will be but as a dead carcase without a living soul; for tell him, when I am from my Lord,
I withering vade, as flowers from Sun sight;
His presence is to me, as Heavens light.

[**AFFECTIONATA** Exit.

1ST GENTLEMAN
'Tis strange that such an honour cannot perswade a boy!

2ND GENTLEMAN
That proves him a boy, for if he had been at mans estate, he would not have refused it, but have been ambitious of it, and proud to receive it.

1ST GENTLEMAN
Indeed youth is foolish, and knows not how to chose.

2ND GENTLEMAN
When he comes to be a man, he will repent the folly of his youth.

[Exeunt.

SCENE IV

[Enter the **LADY BASHFULL**, and **LADY WAGTAILE** not knowing **SIR SERIOUS DUMB** could speak.

LADY WAGTAILE
Pray Madam, let me perswade you, not to cast your self away, to marry a dumb man, for by my troth, all those that are dumb, are meer fools; for who can be witty or wise that cannot speak, or will not speak, which is as bad.

LADY BASHFULL
Why Madam? wisdom nor wit, doth noth not live nor lye in words, for prudence, fortitude and temperance, expresses wisdom and capacity; ingenuity and fancie expresseth wit, and not words.

LADY WAGTAILE
But let me advise you to chose Sir Humphry Bold, he is worth a thousand of Sir Serious Dumb; besides, he is a more learned man by half, and speaks several Languages.

LADY BASHFULL
Perchance so, and yet not so wise; for Parrots will learn Languages, and yet not know how to be wise, nor what wisdom is, which is to have a sound judgement, a clear understanding, and a prudent forecast.

LADY WAGTAILE
Faith all the World will condemn you to have no forecast, if you marry Sir Serious Dumb.

LADY BASHFULL
Let them speak their worst, I care not, as not fearing their censures.

LADY WAGTAILE
You were fearfull and bashfull.

LADY BASHFULL
'Tis true, but now am grown so confident with honest love, I care not if all the World did know of it; nay, I wish it were published to all ears.

[The **LADY BASHFULL** offers to go away.

LADY WAGTAILE
Nay, you must not go, untill you have granted my suit in the behalf of Sir Humphry Bold.

LADY BASHFULL
Pray let me go, for I hate him more, than Heaven hates Hell.

LADY WAGTAILE
Nay, then I will leave you.

[Exeunt.

SCENE V

[Enter **AFFECTIONATA**, who weeps. Enter the **LORD SINGULARITY**.

LORD SINGULARITY
Why weepest thou Affectionata?

AFFECTIONATA
Alas, my Lord, I am in such a passion, as I shall dye, unless
it flows forth thorough mine eyes, and runs from off my tongue.
For like as vapours from the Earth doth rise,
And gather into clouds beneath the skies;
Contracts to water, swelling like moist veins,
When over-fill'd, falls down in showering rains:
So thoughts, which from a grieved mind are sent,
Ariseth in a vaporous discontent:
Contracts to melancholly, which heavy lies
Untill it melts, and runs forth through the eyes;
Unless the Sun of comfort, dry doth drink
Those watery tears that lyes at the eyes brink;

Or that the rayes of joy, which streams bright out
With active heat disperseth them about.

LORD SINGULARITY
Faith Affectionata, I am no good Poet, but thy passion moves so sweetly in numbers and stops, so just
with rhimes, as I cannot but answer thee,
Like as the Sun beauty streams rayes about,
A smiling countenance like day breaks out:
And though a frown obscures sweet beauties sight,
Yet beauties beams makes cloudy frowns more bright:
But melancholly beauty doth appear
As pleasing shades, or Summers evenings clear.
So doth thine Affectionata, but prethee do not wast thy breath into sighs, nor distill thy life into tears.

AFFECTIONATA
I wish I might here breath my last, and close my eyes for ever.

LORD SINGULARITY
I perceive Affectionata, you take it unkindly I did perswade you to take the Dukes offer; But if you think I
did it out of any other design than a true affection to you; By Heaven, you do me wrong by false
interpretation.

AFFECTIONATA
If you, my Lord, did love but half so well as I, you would rather chose to dye, than part with me.

LORD SINGULARITY
I love thee beyond my own interest or delight, for what is best for thee, I account as the greatest
blessing, should it bring me any other wayes a curse.

AFFECTIONATA
Then let me still live with you, for that is best for me.

LORD SINGULARITY
Here I do vow to Heaven, to do my indeavour with my life to keep thee with me, or to be alwayes where
thou art.

AFFECTIONATA
O! what a weight you have taken from my soul, wherein my thoughts like wet-winged-birds sate heavy;
my senses like as blinking Lamps which vaporous damps of grief had neer put out.

LORD SINGULARITY
Let me tell thee Affectionata, I have travelled far, observed much, and have had divers incounters, but I
never met such vertue, found such truth, nor incountered such an affection as thine.

[Imbraces him.

And thus I do imbrace thee, and do wish our souls may twine,
As our each bodyes thus together joyn.

[Exeunt.

[Enter **SIR SERIOUS DUMB**, and his Mistriss the **LADY BASHFULL**.

SIR SERIOUS DUMB
Dear Mistriss, do not you repent your favours, and wish your promise were never made; doth not your affection vade?

LADY BASHFULL
No, it cannot, for never was any love placed upon a Nobler soul than my love is, which is on yours, insomuch, as I do glory in my affection, and grow self-conceited of its judgement.

SIR SERIOUS DUMB
And will you be constant?

LADY BASHFULL
Let not your humble thoughts raise a doubt of jealousie; for I am fixt, as time is to eternity.

SIR SERIOUS DUMB
Then I thank nature for your Creation, honour for your Breeding, and heaven for your Vertue, and fortune that hath given you to me, for I can own nothing of that worth that could deserve you.

LADY BASHFULL
I cannot condemn jealousie, because it proceeds from pure love, and love melts into kinds on a constant heart, but flames like Oyle on a false one, which sets the whole life on fire

SIR SERIOUS DUMB
But now I cannot doubt your love nor constancies, since you have promised your heart to me; for true Lovers are like the light and the Sun, inseparable.

[Exeunt.

[Enter some **COMMANDERS**.

1ST COMMANDER
Come fellow-souldiers, are you ready to march?

2ND COMMANDER
Whether?

1ST COMMANDER
Into our own native Country, for our General is sent for home.

3RD COMMANDER
Except there be wars in our own Country, we cannot go with him.

1ST COMMANDER
I know not whether there be wars or peace, but he obeys, for he is preparing for his journey.

2ND COMMANDER
Who shall be General when he is gone?

3RD COMMANDER
I know not, but I hear the States offers to make our young Lieutenant-General, General, but he refuseth it.

2ND COMMANDER
Would they would make me General?

3RD COMMANDER
If thou wert General, thou wouldst put all method out of order.

1ST COMMANDER
Faith Gentlemen, I would lead you most prudently, and give you leave to plunder most unanimously. And we would fight couragiously, to keep what we plunder.

2ND COMMANDER
Come, let us go, and inquire how our affairs goeth.

[Exeunt.

SCENE VIII

[Enter the **LORD SINGULARITY**, and **AFFECTIONATA**.

LORD SINGULARITY
Now Affectionata, we have taken our leave of the States:
I hope thy mind is at peace, and freed from fears of being staid.

AFFECTIONATA
Yes my Lord.

LORD SINGULARITY
They did perswade thee much to stay.

AFFECTIONATA
They seemed much troubled for your Lordships departure.

LORD SINGULARITY
Truly I will say thus much for my self, that I have done them good service, and I must say thus much for them, that they have rewarded me well.

AFFECTIONATA
I have heard, my Lord, that States seldom rewards a service done; wherefore I believe, they hope you will return again, and sees you for that end.

LORD SINGULARITY
I shall not be unwilling when my Country hath no imployment for me.

AFFECTIONATA
Methinks, my Lord, since you have gotten a fame abroad, you should desire to live a setled life at home.

LORD SINGULARITY
A setled life would seem but dull to me that hath no wife nor children.

AFFECTIONATA
You may have both, If you please, my Lord.

LORD SINGULARITY
For children I desire none, since I have thee, and wives I care not for, but what are other mens.

[Enter a **MESSENGER** with a Letter to the **LORD SINGULARITY**.

LORD SINGULARITY
From whence comest thou friend?

MESSENGER
From Rome, my Lord.

LORD SINGULARITY
If you please to stay in the next room, I shall speak to you presently.

[**MESSENGER** Exit.

[The **LORD SINGULARITY** breaks up the Letter and reads.

LORD SINGULARITY
Affectionata, From whence do you think this Letter comes?

AFFECTIONATA
I cannot guess, my Lord.

LORD SINGULARITY

From the Pope, who hath heard so much of thy youth, vertue, wit and courage, as he desires me to pass thorough Rome im my journey home, that he might see thee.

AFFECTIONATA
Pray Heaven his Holynesse doth not put me into a Monastery, and force me to stay behind you.

LORD SINGULARITY
If he should, I will take the habit, and be incloistered with thee; but he will not inforce a youth that hath no will thereto.

AFFECTIONATA
Truly my Lord, I have no will to be a Fryer.

LORD SINGULARITY
Indeed it is somewhat too lazie a life, which all heroick Spirits shames, for those loves liberty and action: But I will go and dispatch this Messenger, and to morrow we will begin our journey.

[Exeunt.

SCENE IX

[Enter the **LADY WAGTAILE**, and the **LADY AMOROUS**.

LADY WAGTAILE
Faith Amorous, it had been a victory indeed worth the bragging off, if we could have taken Sir Peaceable Studious Loves prisoner, and could have infettered him in Cupid 's bonds.

LADY AMOROUS
It had been a victory indeed, for I will undertake to inslave five Courtiers, and ten Souldiers, sooner, and in less time than one studious Scholar.

LADY WAGTAILE
But some Scholars are more easily taken than the luxurious Courtiers, or deboist Souldiers.

LADY AMOROUS
O no! for Luxurie and Rapine begets lively Spirits, but a study quenches them out.

LADY WAGTAILE
One would think so by Sir Peaceable Studious, but not by some other Scholars that I am acquainted with.

LADY AMOROUS
But confess, Lady Wagtail, do not you find a studious Scholar dull company, in respect of a vain Courtier, and a rough Souldier.

LADY WAGTAILE

must confess, they that study Philosophy, are little too much inclined to morality, but those that study Theologie, are not so restringent.

LADY AMOROUS
Well, for my part, since I have been acquainted with Sir Peaceable Studious, I hate all Scholars.

[Exeunt.

SCENE X

[Enter **THREE MEN**, as the Inhabitants of Rome.

1ST MAN
Tis a wonder such a youth as the Lord Singularity 's Son is, should have so great a wit, as to be able to dispute with so many Cardinals.

2ND MAN
The greater wonder is, that he should have the better of them!

1ST MAN
'Tis said the Pope doth admire him! and is extreamly taken with him.

2ND MAN
If Jove had so much admired him, he would have made him his Ganimed.

1ST MAN
He offered to make him a living Saint, but he thanked his Holyness, and said, he might Saint him, but not make him holy enough to be a Saint, for said he, I am unfit to have Prayers offered to me, that cannot offer Prayers as I ought, or live as I should; then he offered him a Cardinals hat, but he refused it; saying he was neither wise enough, nor old enough for to accept of it; for said he, I want Ulisses head, and Nestors years to be a Cardinal, for though less devotion will serve a Cardinal than a Saint, yet politick wisdom is required.

3RD MAN
Pray Neighbours tell me which way, and by what means I may see this wonderfull youth; for I have been out of the Town, and not heard of him.

2ND MAN
You cannot see him now, unless you will follow him where he is gone.

1ST MAN
Why, whether is he gone?

2ND MAN
Into his own Country, and hath been gone above this week.

3RD MAN
Nay, I cannot follow him thither.

[Exeunt.

[Enter the **LORD SINGULARITY**, and **AFFECTIONATA**, as being in the Country.

LORD SINGULARITY
Affectionata, you have promised me to be ruled by me in every thing, so that you may not part from me.

AFFECTIONATA
I have, my Lord, and will obey all your commands, so far as I am able.

LORD SINGULARITY
Then I am resolved now I am returned into my own Country, to get thee a wife, that thy fame and worthy acts may live in thy Posterity.

AFFECTIONATA
Jove bless me, a wife! by Heaven, my Lord, I am not man enough to marry!

LORD SINGULARITY
There is many as young as you, that have been Fathers, and have had children.

AFFECTIONATA
If they were such as I am, they might father Children, but never get them.

LORD SINGULARITY
Thou art modest, Affectionata, but I will have you marry, and I will chose thee such a wife, as modest as thy self.

AFFECTIONATA
Then we never shall have children, Sir.

LORD SINGULARITY
Love and acquaintance will give you confidence; but tell me truly, Affectionata, didst thou never court a Mistriss?

AFFECTIONATA
No truly, Sir.

LORD SINGULARITY

Well, I will have you practice Courtship, and though I will not directly be your Baud or Pimp, yet I will send you amongst the effeminate Sex, where you may learn to sport with Ladies, as well as fight with Turks.

AFFECTIONATA [Speaks softly to her self]
Pray, Jove they do not search me.

[Exeunt.

SCENE XII

[Enter the **LADY WAGTAIL**, and the **LADY AMOROUS**.

LADY WAGTAILE
I can tell you news?

LADY AMOROUS
What news?

LADY WAGTAILE
Sir Serious Dumb can speak again!

LADY AMOROUS
I am sorrow for that, for now he may tell tales out of School.

LADY WAGTAILE
If he do, we will whip him with the rods of tongues, which is more sharp than the rods of wyer.

LADY AMOROUS
We may whip him with words, but we our selves shall feel the smart of reproch.

LADY WAGTAILE
How simply you talk, as if reproch could hurt a woman; when reproch is born with us, and dyes with us.

LADY AMOROUS
If reproch have no power of our Sex, why are all women so carefull to cover their faults, and so fearfull to have their crimes divulged.

LADY WAGTAILE
Out of two reasons; first, because those of the masculine Sex, which have power, as Fathers, Uncles, Brothers and Husbands; would cut their throats, if they received any disgrace by them; for disgrace belongs more to men than women: The other, reason is, that naturally women loves secrets; yet there is nothing they can keep secret, but their own particular faults, neither do they think pleasure sweet, but what is stollen.

LADY AMOROUS

By your favour, women cannot keep their own faults secret.

LADY WAGTAILE
O yes, those faults that may ruine them if divulged, but they cannot keep a secret that is delivered to their trust; for naturally women are unfit for trust, or council.

LADY AMOROUS
But we are fit for faction.

LADY WAGTAILE
The World would be but a dull World, if it were not for industrious factions.

LADY AMOROUS
The truth is, that if it were not for faction, the World would lye in the cradle of Peace, and be rock'd into a quiet sleep of security.

LADY WAGTAILE
Prethee talk not of quiet, and peace, and rest, for I hate them as bad as death.

LADY AMOROUS
Indeed they resemble death, for in death there is no wars nor noise.

LADY WAGTAILE
Wherefore it is natural for life, neither to have rest not peace, being cantrary to death.

[Exeunt.

ACT IV

SCENE I

[Enter the **LORD SINGULARITY**, and **AFFECTIONATA**.

AFFECTIONATA
My Lord, I hear the King hath invited you to attend him in his progress this Summer.

LORD SINGULARITY
Yes, but I have made my excuse, and have got leave to stay at home; for I will tell thee truly, that I had rather march ten miles with an Artillery, than travel one with a Court; and I had rather fight a battel, than be bound to ceremony, or flattery, which must be practised if one live at Court: Besides, I have been bred to lead an Armie, and not to follow a Court; And the custom of the one have made me unacquainted, and so unfit for the other; for though I may truly say I am a good Souldier, yet I will confess ingenuously to thee, I am a very ill Courtier.

AFFECTIONATA
I think they are the most happiest, that are least acquainted with a great Monarchs Court.

LORD SINGULARITY
I will tell thee a discourse upon this theam in the time of Henry the eighth of England, there were many Courtiers of all degrees about him, and the theam of their discourse was, who was the happiest man in England; So all the Nobles and inferiour Courtiers agreed unanimously it was his Majesty, and it could be no man else; and they all said, that their judgements was so clear in that point, that it could not admit of a contradiction, or dispute: Said Henry the eighth, by the body of our Lord, you are all mistaken; then said one of the Courtiers, I beseech your Majesty to tell us who is the happiest man; By the Lord, said the King, that Gentleman that lives to his profit, and dare moderately spend for his pleasure, and that neither knows me, nor I know him, he is the happiest man in the Kingdom; and I am of Henry the eights opinion; but howsoever, it were better to be such a one that goeth with the bagge and baggage of an Armie, than one of the tail of a Court.

AFFECTIONATA
But your Lordship would not refuse to be as the chief, as to be a Favourite; for a Favourite is more sought, feared and flattered, than the King himself.

LORD SINGULARITY
I think I should not refuse to be a Favourite, by reason a Favourite is a General to command, Martial and Conduct in all affairs, both at home and abroad, in peace and in war, and all by the power and authority of the commission of Favourites.

AFFECTIONATA
Which Commission hath a greater and larger extent than any other Commission.

LORD SINGULARITY
You say right, for it extends as far as the Kings power.

[Exeunt

SCENE II

[Enter the **LADY BASHFULL**, and **MRS REFORMER** her woman.

MRS REFORMER
Madam, shall your wedding be private, or publick?

LADY BASHFULL
Private.

MRS REFORMER
I wonder you will have it private.

LADY BASHFULL
Why do you wonder?

MRS REFORMER
Because the wedding-day is the only triumphant day of a young maids life.

LADY BASHFULL
Do you call that a triumphant day, that inslaves a woman all her life after; no, I will make no triumph on that day.

MRS REFORMER
Why, you had better have one day than none.

LADY BASHFULL
If my whole life were triumphant, it would be but as one day when it was past, or rather as no day nor time; for what is past, is as if it never were; and for one day I will never put my self to that ceremonious trouble, which belongs to feasting, revelling, dressing and the like.

MRS REFORMER
I perceive your Ladyship desires to be undrest upon the Wedding-day.

LADY BASHFULL
No, that I do not, but as I will not be carelesly undrest, so I will not be drest for a Pageant show.

[Exeunt.

SCENE III

[Enter the **LORD SINGULARITY**, and **AFFECTIONATA**.

AFFECTIONATA
I think there is no Family more methodically ordered, prudently governed than your Lordships.

LORD SINGULARITY
It were a disgrace to my profession, if I should not well know how to command; for a good Commander in the field, can tell how to be a good Manager in his private Family, although a prudent Master of a Family knows not how to be a skilfull Commander in the field; but a prudent Master must have a trusty Steward, so a knowing General must have a carefull and skilfull Lieutenant-General, or else he will be very much troubled; also both Master and General must have other Officers, or else they will not find their Accounts or Conquests as he hopes or expects; For neither General nor Master can order every particular command, nor rectifie every particular errour himself; for a Generals Office, is only to direct, order and command the chief Officers, and not the common Souldiers: So the Master of a Family, is only to direct, order and command his Steward, he the rest of the Officers, and the common servants, every one must order those that belongs to their several Offices.

AFFECTIONATA
Then the common Servants are like the common Souldiers.

LORD SINGULARITY

They are so, and are as apt to mutiny, if they be not used with strickt discipline: Thus, if a Master of a Family have the right way in the management of his particular affairs, he may thrive easily, have plenty, live peaceably, be happy, and carry an honourable port with an indifferent Estate, when those of much greater Estates, which knows not, nor practices the right method, or rules and governs not with strictness, his servants shall grow factious, mutinous, and be alwaies in bruleries, by which disorders his Estate shall waste invisible, his servants cozen egregiously; he lives in penurie, his servants in riot, alwaies spending, yet alwaies wanting, forced to borrow, and yet hath so much, that if it were ordered with prudence, might be able to lend, when by his imprudence, he is troubled with stores, yet vex'd with necessity.

AFFECTIONATA
I should think that no man ought to be a Master of a Family, but those that can govern orderly and peaceably.

LORD SINGULARITY
You say right, for every Master of a Family are petty-Kings, and when they have rebellions in their own small Monarchies, they are apt to disturb the general Peace of the whole Kingdom or State they live in; for those that cannot tell how to command their own Domesticks, and prudently order their own affairs, are not only uselesse to the Common-wealth, but they are pernicious and dangerous, as not knowing the benefit and necessity of obedience and method.

[Exeunt.

SCENE IV

[Enter the **LADY WAGTAILE**, and the **LADY AMOROUS**.

LADY WAGTAILE
The Lord Singularity hath brought home the sweetest, and most beautifullest young Cavalier, as ever I saw.

LADY AMOROUS
Faith he appears like Adonas.

LADY WAGTAILE
Did you ever see Adonas?

LADY AMOROUS
No, but I have heard the Poets describe him.

LADY WAGTAILE
Venus and Adonas are only two poetical Ideas, or two Ideas in poetical brains.

LADY AMOROUS
Why, Ideas hath no names.

LADY WAGTAILE
O yes, for Poets christens their Ideas with names, as orderly as Christians Fathers doth their children.

LADY AMOROUS
Well, I wish I were a Venus for his sake.

LADY WAGTAILE
But if you were only a poetical Venus, you would have little pleasure with your Adonas.

LADY AMOROUS
Hay ho! He is a sweet youth.

LADY WAGTAILE
And you have sweet thoughts of the sweet youth.

LADY AMOROUS
My thoughts are like Mirtle-groves to entertain the Idea of the Lord Singularity 's Son.

LADY WAGTAILE
Take heed there be not a wild-boar in your Mirtle Imagenarie Grove, that may destroy your Adonas Idea.

LADY AMOROUS
There is no beast there, only sweet singing-birds called Nightingals.

[Exeunt.

SCENE V

[Enter the **LORD SINGULARITY**, and **AFFECTIONATA**.

AFFECTIONATA
Pray, my Lord, what Lady is that you make such inquiry for?

LORD SINGULARITY
She is a Lady I would have thee marry; One that my Father did much desire I should marry, although she was very young, and may be now about thy years. I hear her Father is dead, but where the Lady is, I cannot find out.

AFFECTIONATA
Perchance she is married, my Lord.

LORD SINGULARITY
Then we should find her out, by hearing who she hath marryed.

AFFECTIONATA

But if she be not marryed, she being as old as I, I am too young for her, for Husbands should be older than their wives.

LORD SINGULARITY
But she is one that is well born, well bred, and very rich; and though thou art young in years, yet thou art an aged man in judgment, prudence, understanding, and for wit, as in thy flourishing strength.

AFFECTIONATA
Perchance, my Lord, she will not like me, as neither my years, my person, nor my birth.

LORD SINGULARITY
As for thy years, youth is alwayes accepted by the effeminate Sex; and thy person she cannot dislike, for thou art very handsom, and for thy birth, although thou art meanly born, thou hast a noble nature, a sweet disposition, a vertuous soul, and a heroick spirit; Besides, I have adopted thee my Son, and the King hath promised to place my Titles on thee, and hath made thee Heir of my whole Estate, for to maintain thee according to those Dignities.

AFFECTIONATA
But I had rather live unmarried, my Lord, if you will give consent.

LORD SINGULARITY
But I will never consent to that, and if you be dutifull to me, you will marry such a one as I shall chose for you.

AFFECTIONATA
I shall obey whatsoever you command, for I have nothing but my obedience to return for all your favours.

LORD SINGULARITY
Well, I will go and make a strickt inquiry for this Lady.

[**LORD SINGULARITY** Exit.

[**AFFECTIONATA** alone.

AFFECTIONATA
Hay ho! what will this come to, I would I were in my Grave; for love and fear doth torture my poor life; Heaven strike me dead! or make me this Lords wife.

[Exeunt.

SCENE VI

[Enter the **LADY WAGTAILE**, and the **LADY AMOROUS**.

LADY AMOROUS

How shall we compass the acquaintance of the Lord Singularity 's Son?

LADY WAGTAILE

Faith Amorous, thou lovest boys, but I love men; wherefore I would be acquainted with the Lord Singularity himself; Besides, his adopted Son was a poor Beggar-boy 'tis said, and I cannot love one that is basely born.

LADY AMOROUS

His birth may be honourably, though poor, and of low and mean descent; for if he was born in honest wedlock, and of honest Parents, his birth cannot be base.

LADY WAGTAILE

O yes, for those that are not born from Gentry, are like course brown bread, when Gentry of ancient descent, are like flower often boulted to make white manchet.

LADY AMOROUS

By that rule, surely he came from a Noble and Ancient Race; for I never saw any person more white and finely shap'd in my life than he is; and if fame speaks true, his actions have proved he hath a Gentlemans soul; But say he were meanly born, as being born from a Cottager, yet he is not to be despised nor disliked, nor to be lesse esteemed, or beloved, or to be thought the worse of, for was Lucan lesse esteemed for being a Stone-Cutter, or his wit lesse esteemed; or was King David lesse esteemed or obeyed, for being a Shepheard; or the Apostles lesse esteemed or believed, for being Fisher men, Tent-makers or the like; or the man that was chosen from the Plough, to be made Emperour; I say, was he lesse esteemed for being a Plough-man? No, he was rather admired the more; or was Horace esteemed, or his Poems thought the worse, for being Son to a freed man, which had been a slave; or was Homer lesse admired, or thought the worse Poet, for being a poor blind man, and many hundred that I cannot name, that hath gained fame, and their memories lives with Honour and Admiration in every Age, and in every Nation, Kingdom, Country and Family, and it is more worthy, and those persons ought to have more love and respect, that have merit, than those that have only Dignity, either from favour of Princes, or descended from their Ancestors; for all derived Honours, are poor and mean, in respect of self-creating honour, and they only are to be accounted mean and base, that are so in themselves; but those that are born from low and humble Parents, when they have merits, and have done worthy actions, they are placed higher in fames Court, and hath more honour by fames report, which sounds their praises louder than those of greater descent, although of equal worth and merit, and justly, for it is more praise-worthy, when those that were the lowest, and are as it were trod it to the earth, or was born, as the phrase is; from the Dunghill, should raise themselves equal to the highest, who keeps but where they were placed by birth; but many times they keep not their place, but fall from the Dignity of their birth, into the myer of baseness, treachery and treason, when the other rises as the Sun out of a cloud of darknesse, darting forth glorious beams thorough all that Hemisphere.

LADY WAGTAILE

I perceive by your discourse, Lovers are the best Disputers; Orators, and as I have heard, the best Poets; But I never heard you discourse so well, nor speak so honourably in all my life, wherefore I am confident, 'twas love spake, not you.

[Exeunt.

ACT V

SCENE I

Enter **AFFECTIONATA**, **NURSE FONDLY**, and **FOSTER TRUSTY** her Husband.

NURSE FONDLY
My child, we can no longer conceal you, for we are accused of murthering you, and are summoned to appear before a Judge and Jury.

AFFECTIONATA
For Heaven sake, conceal me as long as you can; for if I be known, I shall be utterly ruined with disgrace.

NURSE FONDLY
Whose fault was it? I did advise you otherwise, but you would not be ruled, nor counselled by me; and my Husband like an unwise man, did assist your childish desires.

FOSTER TRUSTY
Well wife, setting aside your wisdom, let us advise what is best to be done in this case.

NURSE FONDLY
In this case we are either to be hanged, or she is to be disgraced; and for my part, I had rather be hanged, for I am old, and cannot live long.

FOSTER TRUSTY
If you were a young wench, thou mightest chance to escape hanging, the Judges would have taken pity on thee, but being old, will condemn thee without mercy.

NURSE FONDLY
If I were not a pretty wench, and the Jurie amorous men, at least the Judges so, I should be hanged neverthelesse.

AFFECTIONATA
Come, come, Foster Father, and Nurse, let us go and advise.

[Exeunt.

SCENE II

Enter the **LADY WAGTAILE**, and a **CAPTAIN**.

LADY WAGTAILE
Pray tell me, what manner of Country is Italy?

CAPTAIN

In short, Madam, there is more Summer than Winter, more Fruit than Meat, and more meat than Hospitality.

LADY WAGTAILE
Why Captain, fruit is meat.

CAPTAIN
I mean flesh-meat.

LADY WAGTAILE
Out upon that Country, that hath neither Flesh nor Hospitality! But Captain, what are the natures, dispositions, and manners of the Italians?

CAPTAIN
In general, Madam, thus, their natures, dispositions, and manners are, as generally all other people of every other Nation are, for the generality of every Nation are alike, in natures, dispositions and persons; that is, some are of good, and some are of bad, some handsom, and some ill-favoured; but for the most part, there are more ill-favoured than handsom, more soul than fair, and the general manner of the whole World is, to offer more than present, to promise more than perform, to be more faigning than real, more courtly than friendly, more treacherous than trusty, more covetous than generous, and yet more prodigal than covetous; but as for the Italians, they are more luxurious than gluttonous, and they love pleasures more than Heaven.

LADY WAGTAILE
They have reason, by my troth; for who can tell whether in loves Mansion, there are so many sweet and delightfull pleasures, as in this World: But Captain, you do not tell me what pleasure the women have in Italy?

CAPTAIN
Those women that are married, are restrain'd and barr'd from all courtly pleasure, or as I may say, the pleasure of Courtships; but the Courtezans have liberty to please themselves, and to be their own carvers.

LADY WAGTAILE
And there is nothing I love so well, as to carve both for my self and others.

CAPTAIN
And there is no Nation in the World, so curious, and ingenuous in the art of carving, as the Italians.

LADY WAGTAILE
I am resolved to go into Italy, if it be but to learn the art of carving, but I will leave my Husband behind me; for you say, wives have not that free liberty of carving, and if I leave my Husband, I may pass for a Widow, though not for a Maid.

CAPTAIN
But Madam, you are past your travelling years, for the best time for women to travel, is about twenty.

LADY WAGTAILE

By your favour, Sir, a woman never grows old, if she can but conceal her age, and say she is young.

CAPTAIN
But she must often repeat it.

LADY WAGTAILE
She must so, which she may easily do, talking much, for women wants not words, neither are we sparing of them; But Captain, I must intreat your company, for you are acquainted with the Country, and hath the experience of the humours and natures of that people, and having been a Souldier and a Traveller, will not be to seek in the wayes of our journey.

CAPTAIN
I shall wait upon you, Madam.

LADY WAGTAILE
No Captain, you shall be as Master, to command, and I will be your Servant to obey.

CAPTAIN
You shall command me, Madam.

[Exeunt.

SCENE III

Enter **AFFECTIONATA** sola.

O! How my soul is tormented with love, shame, grief and fear (she stops a little) I am in love, but am ashamed to make it known, Besides, I have given the World cause to censure me, not only in concealing of my Sex, and changing of my habit, but being alwaies in the company of Men, acting a masculine part upon the Worlds great Stage, and to the publick view; but could I live thus concealed, I should be happy, and free from censure: But O curst fortune! that pleasure takes in crossing Lovers, and basic time that makes all things as restless as it self, doth strive for to divulge my acts, when I have no defence, or honest means for to conceal them; for if I do oppose, I shall become a Murtherer, and bear a guilty conscience to my grave, which may torment my soul, when as my body is turn'd to dust.

[Stops.

But since there is no remedy, i'l weep my sorrows forth, and with the water of my tears, i'l strive to quench the blushing heat, that like quick lightening, flashes in my face.

[Enter the Lord Singularity, finding Affectionata Weeping.

LORD SINGULARITY
My dear Affectionata,
What makes thee so melancholly, as to be alwaies weeping?

AFFECTIONATA

I must confess, my Lord, here of late my eyes have been like Egypt, when it is over-flown with Nilus, and all my thoughts like Crockodiles.

LORD SINGULARITY

What is the cause?

AFFECTIONATA

Alas, my Lord, causes lyes so obscure, they are seldom found.

LORD SINGULARITY

But the effects may give us light to judge what causes are.

AFFECTIONATA

Effects deceives, and often cozens us, by reason one effect may be produced from many several causes, and several effects proceeds from one cause.

LORD SINGULARITY

But thy tears seems as if they were produced from some passion.

AFFECTIONATA

Indeed they are produced from passions and appetites, for passions are the rayes of the mind, and appetites the vapour of the senses, and the rayes of my mind hath drawn up the vapour of my senses into thick moist clouds, which falls in showering tears.

LORD SINGULARITY

Tell me thy griefs, and thy desires, that I may help the one, and ease the other.

AFFECTIONATA

Alas, my Lord, I cannot, for they lye in the conceptions; and conceptions ariseth like mysts, and my thoughts like clouds, lyes one above another.

LORD SINGULARITY

Come, come, let reason the Sun of the soul verifie those misty conceptions, and disperse this dull humour, that the mind may be clear, and the thoughts serene.

AFFECTIONATA

I will strive to bring in the light of mirth.

[Exeunt.

SCENE IV

Enter the **LADY WAGTAILE**, the **LADY AMOROUS**, and **SIR HUMPHREY BOLD**.

LADY WAGTAILE

Good Sir Humphry Bold, carry us to the Court of Iudicatures, to hear the great Tryal, which is said to be to day.

SIR HUMPHREY BOLD
You would go to hear the condemnation of an old man, and his old wife.

LADY WAGTAILE
No, we would go to hear the confessions, as whether they have murthered the young Lady that is missing, or not.

SIR HUMPHREY BOLD
Why, that you may hear from other relations, as well as from their own mouths, and so save you so much pains and trouble, as you will have to get a place, and to stand so long a time, as the examining, accusing, confessing, freeing, or condemning, which will require so long a time, as Ladies will find great inconveniencies, and be put mightily to it.

LADY WAGTAILE
But I long to hear and see the manner of it.

SIR HUMPHREY BOLD
I will wait upon you, but you will be very much crouded.

LADY AMOROUS
I had rather see them hanged, if they be guilty, than hear them judged and condemned.

SIR HUMPHREY BOLD
Why, a condemning Judge is the chief Hang-man, for he hangs with his word, as the other with a cord.

LADY WAGTAILE
Will the Lord Singularity be there?

SIR HUMPHREY BOLD
Yes certainly, for he is the man that doth accuse them.

LADY AMOROUS
And will his Son be there?

SIR HUMPHREY BOLD
I know not that.

[Exeunt.

SCENE V

Enter the **JUDGES** and **JURY-MEN**, as in a Court of Judicature; the **LORD SINGULARITY**, **FOSTER TRUSTY**, and **NURSE FONDLY**, and many **OTHERS** to hear them.

JUDGES
Who accuses these persons of murther?

LORD SINGULARITY
I, my Lord.

FOSTER TRUSTY
We beseech your Honours, not to condemn us before you have found us guilty.

LORD SINGULARITY
It is a proof sufficient, my Lord, they cannot clear themselves, or produce the party that was delivered to their trust and care.

JUDGES
Jurie, do you find them guilty or not?

JURIES
Guilty, my Lord.

JUDGES
Then from the Jurie, we can—.

[Enter **AFFECTIONATA**, drest very sine in her own Sexes habit, and stops the **JUDGES** sentence.

AFFECTIONATA
Hold, condemn not these innocent persons for their fidelity, constancy and love; I am that maid they are accused to murther, and by good circumstances can prove it.

[All the **ASSEMBLY**, **JUDGES** and **JURIE**, seems as in a maze at her beauty, and slares on her. The **LORD SINGULARITY**, as soon as he seeth her, starts back, then goeth towards her, his eyes all the time sixt on her; speaking as to himself.

LORD SINGULARITY
Sure it is that face.

[He takes her by the Hand, and turns her to the light

Are not you my Affectionata, whom I adopted my Son.

AFFECTIONATA
Shame stops my breath, and chokes the words I should utter.

LORD SINGULARITY
For Heaven sake speak quickly, release my fears, or crown my joyes.

AFFECTIONATA

My Lord, pray pardon loves follies, and condemn not my modesty for dissembling my Sex; for my designs were harmless, as only to follow you as a servant: For by Heaven, my Lord? my only desire was, that my eyes, and my eares might be fed with the sight of your person, and sound of your voice, which made me travel to hear, and to see you: But since I am discovered, I will otherwise conceal my self, and live as an Anchoret from the view of the World.

LORD SINGULARITY

Pray let me live with you.

AFFECTIONATA

That may not be, for an Anchoret is to live alone.

LORD SINGULARITY

If you will accept of me for your husband, we shall be as one.

AFFECTIONATA

You have declared against marriage, my Lord.

LORD SINGULARITY

I am converted, and shall become so pious a devote, as I shall offer at no Alter but Hymens, and since I am your Convert, refuse me not.

AFFECTIONATA

I love too well to refuse you.

[He kneels down on one knee, and kisses her hand.

LORD SINGULARITY

Here on my knee I do receive you as a blessing, and a gift from the Gods.

[He riseth.

AFFECTIONATA

Most Reverend Judges, and Grave Jury, sentence me not with censure, nor condemn me to scandals, for waiting as a Man, and serving as a Page; For though I dissembled in my outward habit and behaviour, yet I was alwaies chaste and modest in my nature.

[Exeunt.

SCENE VI

Enter the **LADY WAGTAILE**, and **LADY AMOROUS**.

LADY WAGTAILE

Now Lady Amorous, is your mind a Mirtel-grove, and your thoughts Nightingals to entertain the Idea of your Adonas.

LADY AMOROUS

Her discovery hath proved the boar that kill'd him; but I desire much to be army Adonas Funeral, which is the Lady Orphants wedding.

LADY WAGTAILE

I am acquainted with some of the Lord Singularity's Captains and Officers, and I will speak to some of them to speak to the Lord Singularity to invite us.

LADY AMOROUS

I pray do, for since my Adonas is dead, I will strive to inamour Mars, which is the Lord Singularity himself.

LADY WAGTAILE

Faith, that is unfriendly done, for I have laid my designs for himself.

LADY AMOROUS

I fear both of our designs may come to nothing, he is so inamoured with his own She-Page, or female Son.

[Exeunt.

SCENE VII

Enter **NURSE FONDLY**, and **FOSTER TRUSTY**.

NURSE FONDLY

O Husband! This is the joyfullest day that ever I had in my whole life, except at mine own wedding.

FOSTER TRUSTY

Indeed, this day is a day of Iubile.

NURSE FONDLY

Of Iuno, say you; but Husband, have you provided good chear, and enough; for here are a world of Guests come, more than was invited, and you being Master Steward, will be thought too blame, if there be any thing wanting.

FOSTER TRUSTY

If you be as carefull to dress the Brides Chamber, as I to provide for the bridal Guest, you nor I shall be in a fault.

NURSE FONDLY

I saith, if you have done your part, as I have done my part, we shall deserve praise.

FOSTER TRUSTY

I saith, we are almost so old, that we are almost past praise.

NURSE FONDLY
None can merit praise, but those in years; for all Worthy, Noble and Heroick Acts requires time to do them, and who was ever wise, that was young?

FOSTER TRUSTY
And few are praised that are old, for as fame divulgeth merits, so time wears out praise, for time hath more power than fame, striving to destroy what fame desires to keep. The truth is, time is a Glutton, for he doth not only strive to destroy what fame divulgeth, but what himself begets and produceth.

[Exeunt.

SCENE VIII

Enter the **LORD SINGULARITY**, and the **LADY ORPHANT**, as Bride and Bride-groom, and a company of **BRIDAL-GUESTS**. Enter **MUSICIANS**, and meets them.

MUSICIANS
We desire your Excellence will give us leave to present you with a Song written by my Lord Marquiss of New-Castle.

LORD SINGULARITY
Your present could have never been less acceptable, by reason it will retard my marriage.

LADY ORPHANT
Pray, my Lord, hear them.

LORD SINGULARITY
Come, come, dispatch, dispatch.

[He seems not to listen to them. All the time his eyes fixt on the Bride.

SONG
Love in thy younger age,
Thou then turn'd Page;
When love then stronger grew,
The bright sword drew.
Then Love it was thy fate
To advise in State.
My Love adopted me
His childe to be.
Then offered was my hap
A Cardinals Cap.
Loves juglings thus doth make
The Worlds mistake.

LORD SINGULARITY
By Heaven, Musitioners, you are all so dillotarie with your damnable and harsh prologue of tuning before you play, as the next Parliament will make it felony in Fidlers, if not treason, when your Great Royal Eares; begin with a Fare to you.

MUSICIANS
Why, my Noble Lord, we have done.

LORD SINGULARITY
By Heaven, there spake Apollo! Give them ten Pieces.

MUSICIANS
Madam, an Eppilanian! we have more to express our further joy, and then we will pray for blessings on you both.

LORD SINGULARITY
O! It will be my funeral song, you rogues, know all delays doth kill me; and at this time your best Musick sounds harsh, and out of tune.

LADY ORPHANT
Pray let them sing that one song more; so ends your trouble of them.

LORD SINGULARITY
Begin, quick, quick.

SONG
O Love, some says thou art a Boy!
But now turn'd Girl, thy Masters joy.
Now cease all thy fierce alarms,
In circles of your loving arms.
Who can express the joys to night,
'Twil charm your senses with delight,
Nay, all those pleasures you'l controul,
With joyning your each soul to soul.
Thus in Loves raptures live, till you
Melting, dissolv into a dew;
And then your aery journey take,
So both one constellation make.

[The Song done, the Musick playes, as the Bride and Bridegroom goeth.

Margaret Cavendish – A Concise Bibliography

Philosophical Fancies (1653)
Poems and Fancies (1653)
Philosophical and Physical Opinions (1655)

Nature's Pictures drawn by Fancie's Pencil to the Life (1656)
The World's Olio (1655)
Playes, (1662) folio, containing twenty-one plays including
Loves Adventures
The Several Wits
Youths Glory, and Deaths Banquet
The Lady Contemplation
Wits Cabal
The Unnatural Tragedy
The Public Wooing
The Matrimonial Trouble
Nature's Three Daughters, Beauty, Love and Wit
The Religious
The Comical Hash
Bell in Campo
A Comedy of the Apocryphal Ladies
The Female Academy
Plays never before printed (1668), containing five plays.
The Sociable Companions, or the Female Wits
The Presence
The Bridals
The Convent of Pleasure
A Piece of a Play
Orations of Divers Sorts (1662)
Philosophical Letters, or Modest Reflections upon some Opinions in Natural Philosophy maintained by several learned authors of the age (1664)
CCXI Sociable Letters (1664)
Observations upon Experimental Philosophy & Description of a New World (1666)
The Blazing World (1666)
The Life of William Cavendish, Duke, Marquis, and Earl of Newcastle, Earl of Ogle, Viscount Mansfield, and Baron of Bolsover, of Ogle, Bothal, and Hepple, &c. (1667)
Grounds of Natural Philosophy (1668)

www.ingramcontent.com/pod-product-compliance
Lightning Source LLC
Chambersburg PA
CBHW021943040426
42448CB00008B/1216